LARRY CULLIFORD

the little book of
WISDOM

A POCKET GUIDE TO
LIVING WELL

Hero, 51 Gower Street, London, WC1E 6HJ
hero@hero-press.com | www.hero-press.com

Contents © Larry Culliford 2021
The right of the above author to be identified as the author of this work
has been asserted in accordance with the Copyright, Designs and Patents
Act 1988. British Library Cataloguing in Publication Data available.

Print ISBN 978-1-80031-3-736
Ebook ISBN 978-1-80031-3-743
Set in Times. Printed by Lightning Source.

Dr Larry Culliford trained in medicine at St Catharine's College, Cambridge and Guy's Hospital, London. He worked in hospital medicine and general practice in UK, New Zealand and Australia, and later qualified as a psychiatrist, working until retirement in the UK National Health Service. He has published numerous books and articles on happiness, psychology and spirituality.

Visit Larry at
www.LDC52.co.uk

PREFACE

People everywhere are experiencing highly disturbing effects from the Covid-19 pandemic. Unfortunately, the deadly infection arrived during an already worrying period of climate change, eco-destruction, environmental pollution, increasing natural disasters, widespread conflict, a refugee crisis and many other causes of human suffering. Happily, however, there is a bold and effective remedy for the pain attached to society's far-reaching ailments… a solution summed up in a single word – *wisdom*.

Wisdom basically means knowing how to live well for *both* self *and* others. Reflecting on that idea will hopefully prompt a few people towards both learning about, and growing in, wisdom. That is the hoped-for aim of this little book. It can be used as a pocket guide to dip into from time to time; but I recommend starting with a read through from first to last page, reading and rereading, slowly and carefully, while experiencing the ideas accumulating and building on each other to become huge life-affirming waves that crash sweetly and gently upon the shoreline of consciousness. It may be best, too, to pause from time to time, allowing these short messages of wisdom gradually to sink in.

Sounding strange, possibly counterintuitive and even disconcerting, it is not necessary to understand, agree with or be attracted to all the ideas you read here right away, only to let them wash lightly through your mind, while absorbing them into your heart. In this way, they begin influencing subtly who you are *and* who you are becoming. As this occurs, readers are sure to benefit; and not only you, but also everyone you interact with and influence in turn. Little by little, you discover yourself growing wiser, calmer and increasingly joyful, contributing as you go towards a safer, cleaner, more peaceful, much happier world. What could be better than that?

Larry Culliford
West Sussex,
January 2021

HEADINGS

TWO KINDS OF KNOWLEDGE

1. There are two kinds of knowledge,
   Science and *Wisdom*...
       ... Both are precious, of great value...
          ... And both worth much effort to obtain.

2. Science is the knowledge of facts...
       ... Of things, and how they work.
   Wisdom is the knowledge of how to live well...
       ... Both for yourself and for other people.

3. It is good to study science and the methods of science.
   It is equally beneficial to study wisdom...
       ... Explore its ways...
          ... Seeking both to know and to grow.

4.   Science speaks of fragments, the parts of things…
         … And their interactions.
      Wisdom reflects things entire…
         … In seamless relationship…
              … With the Whole.

5.   Science is *worldly* knowledge…
         … Earth-bound,
      Constrained by time…
         … And space.

6.   Wisdom is *sacred* knowledge…
         … Unbounded…
              … Limitless…
                   … Eternal.

7.   Sacred means *inviolable*…
         … Untouched by human opinions and preferences.
      The sacred is persuasive and powerful…
         … Beyond analysis and dispute.

FIVE DIMENSIONS

8. The sum of human experience and understanding...
    ... Is covered by just five connected 'dimensions':
    Physical... Biological...
    ... Psychological... Social...
    ... And Spiritual.

9. Science deals with energy and matter – the *physical* dimension...
    ... With organs and organisms – the *biological* dimension,
    With mental activity – the *psychological* dimension...
    ... And with human relationships – the *social* dimension.

10. Wisdom deals with souls and the sacred...
    ... The *spiritual* dimension...
    ... Underpinning, creating...
    ... Linking and shaping...
    ... The other four,

11. The spiritual perspective…

    … Transforms scientific understanding…

        … Of lifeless mechanisms…

            … Into living wonder.

12. Each dimension evokes a miracle.

    The miracle of *existence*…

    … Of how energy and matter, space and time, are related…

        … Forms the territory of *physics* and *chemistry*.

13. The miracle of *life*…

    … Of the wondrous diversity of plants and animals,

    Is explored through *biology*, both botany and zoology…

    … (Which also need mention dying, death, and decay).

14. The miracle of *consciousness*…

    … Of reasoned thought and calculation…

        … Of emotions, painful and joyful…

            … Of impulses to act, and sense perceptions,

    Is revealed through the study of *psychology*.

15. And the miracle of *love*…

    … Of human relations, both at their best…

        … And, sadly, when also they go awry,

            Is approached through anthropology

    And the additional *social sciences*…

16. Finally, the miracle of *cosmic unity*…

    … Is given life in the *spiritual* dimension

    Spirituality, binding the five realms together…

    … Bearing supreme witness to the Oneness of creation.

WISDOM AND THE SPIRIT OF UNITY

17. Wisdom depends, above all, on this sacred unity…

    … On the seamless totality of existence.

    Concerned with wholeness and healing…

    … For healing means 'making whole'…

18. The original meaning of *'spirit'* …

    … Was simply 'breath' or 'wind'.

    So wisdom is like a cosmic breath…

    … A great universal wind.

19. The spiritual realm we inhabit…

    … Is a breathing organism…

    … Home to a great wind…

    … A mysterious life force…

    … That brings everything into being.

20. Our spiritual dwelling-place, the universe…

    … Is filled with vast, invisible energy…

        … That shapes creation…

            … And propels us along…

                … Like a wind.

21. Can we learn to ride the breezes and blusters…

    … Like sailors on the ocean of life?

The simple answer to this question is…

    … 'Yes'.

22. We can learn its eddies and currents…

    … Prepare for violent storms…

        … And the frustrations…

            … Of being becalmed.

23. We can revel…

    … In its awesome power…

        … And grow to love…

            … Its breath-taking beauty.

24. Free from our initial terror…

    … Gradually, we may befriend…

        … The insuperable power…

            … At the heart of creation.

25. Growing in confidence…

    … We can feel it loving us too…

        … Like a mother watching over…

            … Her children, in the dark.

26. Reflecting the magnificent totality…

    … We call wisdom sacred.

    Embodying wholeness…

    … We call it *holy*…

        … Linking our souls to the divine.

KINSHIP

27. You do not have to believe in God...

    ... To know this...

        ... You have only...

            ... To feel alive.

28. You have only...

    ... To experience connection...

        ... Feel a heartfelt bond with earth and nature...

            ... With the entirety of the cosmos.

29. You have only to feel also...

    ... The deepest kinship with your fellow travellers...

        ... Companions together...

            ... On life's rich pilgrimage journey.

30. You have only…

    … To feel love and compassion…

        … For all that is…

                … And for all that will be.

31. Whenever we enjoy the experience of self…

    … As inseparable from the sacred Whole…

        … And feel affection for every aspect and element,

That is when wisdom arrives.

32. Feeling *deeply*, our individual destiny…

    … As *inescapably* bound up…

        … With that of everyone else…

                … Living, deceased, and to come,

That is when wisdom dawns.

33. How may we recognise wisdom?

By experiencing, even briefly…

    … A profound and comforting sense of belonging…

        … Knowing the joy of feeling somehow…

            … That we are being led home.

BELONGING

34. Wisdom brings…

    … The most heartfelt sense of belonging…

        … To all that is…

            … To all that ever was…

                … To all that is yet to come.

35. Always…

    … We have always belonged…

        … And will always belong…

            … To the precious galaxies, stars, sun, moon…

                … And our beautiful, delicate planet.

36. Men and women…

    … Young and old…

        … Dark and fair…

            … For evermore…

                … We belong to each other.

37. Knowing that, irrevocably, we belong to each other...

    ... Through a wondrously warm sense of kinship...

        ... In our hearts, minds, and souls,

This is the origin of wisdom.

38. Remember...

    ... Where there is wholeness...

        ... There can be no division.

Despite differences (of age, gender, race, creed or anything)...

    ... Wisdom says, *"All are one"*.

39. "But," I hear some say, "I am not like everybody else".

This is true, but a paradox...

    ... Be patient with it.

We are the same but different (from one perspective)...

    ... Different but the same (from another).

40. In a *worldly* way...

    ... We are different...

        ... In a *spiritual* way...

            ... We are one.

41. We are spiritually one...

    ... Unified.

A single vast family...

    ... We are kin.

42. Being *kin* to one-another…

    … Means we are of one *kind*…

        … Which explains the wisdom of kind-ness…

            … Everything follows from that.

43. We are kin and alike.

    Equally, though…

        … Each is different…

            … Each of us is unique.

TAKING RESPONSIBILITY

44. Because we are different...

    ... With unique personal fortunes and patterns of life,

    It is an error to model oneself too closely on others...

    ... We are mistaken to blindly follow the crowd.

45. Wisdom requires independence...

    ... So we are wise not always to conform...

        ... Learning, most often...

            ... To think, speak, and act...

                ... For ourselves.

46. Wisdom requires independence...

    ... Of thought, speech and action...

        ... But never with selfish motives.

    Wisdom involves taking responsibility...

    ... For what we say and do.

47. Wisdom involves taking responsibility…

    … For the consequences…

        … Of whatever we say and do…

            … That affects other people…

                … Family, friends and community.

48. Wisdom involves taking responsibility…

    … For what we say and do…

        … Equally, for all that we do *not* say…

            … And whatever we may *fail* to do.

49. Wisdom involves responsibility towards people…

    … Also for the effects we have…

        … On our environment…

            … On the planet…

                … And in space.

50. Requiring such levels of responsibility…

    … Wisdom necessarily involves *maturity*.

It means each of us growing naturally…

    … From an unripe state, towards ripening.

51. But we do *not* like thinking…

    … Of ourselves as immature.

Let's think instead, then, of being on a journey…

… Where there is still some way left to go…

    … Each step bringing us nearer to our goal.

WHAT IS WISDOM?

52. According to one definition …
     … *Wisdom is the knowledge of how to be…*
          … *And to behave…*
               … *For the best.*

53. More…
     … Wisdom is the knowledge of how to be…
          … And behave for the best…
               … *For all concerned.*

54. Still more…
     … Wisdom is the knowledge of how to be…
          … And behave for the best, for all concerned…
               … *In any and all situations.*

55. This is well worth repeating…

   … (Perhaps even say it out loud)…

   … *Wisdom is the knowledge of how to be and behave…*

   … For the best… For all concerned…

   …In any and all situations.

56. Why not spend a moment…

   … To reflect now…

   … On these ideas about wisdom?

   Ask yourself sincerely…

   … *'What do I make of it all?'*

57. *"Wisdom is how to be and behave…*

   … For the best, for all concerned…

   … In any and all situations."

   Admittedly, it does *not* sound easy.

KIND INTENTIONS

58. Gaining wisdom sounds difficult...

   ... But, no need for alarm...

      ... Behaviour begins with intention.

   So, wisdom begins with *intending* to do well...

   ... Both for oneself *and* for others.

59. This, hopefully, seems easier...

   ... To start by cultivating, at least...

      ... The *intention* to act kindly...

         ... At all times.

60. If, as it might, forming the intention to do well...

   ... Seems troublesome...

      ... Perhaps even *impossibly* hard...

         ... We will need to work, will we not...

            ... On ourselves?

61. We need to work on ourselves…

    … To make a constant, determined effort…

        … And…

            … We also need guidance.

62. Life's journey goes more smoothly…

    … Towards goals of maturity and wisdom…

        … When we accept responsibility…

            … Seek guidance…

                … And embark upon training.

THE TIME IS NOW

63. Be reassured that working on ourselves…
    … doing so-called *'wisdom exercises'*…
        … Need not be especially tough.
    Staying patient, with perseverance…
    … Progress can be gentle.

64. Patience and perseverance…
    … Are among the basic virtues…
        … Associated with wisdom,
    Personal attributes to acquire…
    … And gradually develop.

65. It is often wise, for example, to observe…
    … To be patient and wait,
    Rather than speak out hastily…
    … Or act too soon.

66. At other times, on the other hand…

    … It is equally wise to catch the moment,

    Speak and act quickly…

    … When an opportunity arises…

        … To prevent further distress.

67. This is why wisdom can be tricky…

    … And takes time to learn.

    It cannot be done in a hurry…

    … But there's no need to fret…

        … About that.

68. Maybe this sounds mysterious, but…

    … While wisdom can sometimes be gained…

        … In an instant of insight…

            … It cannot be learned in a rush.

69. To learn wisdom cannot be hurried…

    … Nevertheless, whether long or short…

        … What remains of your life lies before you…

        … So please…

            … Take your time.

70. No-one knows when death will come…

    … How long we each have left…

... Whether years, months, days, hours, or minutes.

So relax, pace yourself, but use it...

... Please, do not waste any time.

71. Gaining wisdom seems problematic...

    ... And takes time to learn...

        ... So we are supremely wise...

            ... Not to delay.

72. Like it or not...

    ... We cannot exactly tell how long remains...

        ... Whether long or short...

            ... So, the time to seek wisdom...

                ... Is *now*.

INNER GUIDANCE

73. Obviously, we need guidance…
       … But where can a teacher be found?
       When wisdom teachers are scarce…
       … "Be your own teacher", I say…
           … "If nowhere else, look within!"

74. "But where to start?", you reply…
       … Well, think for a moment about this…
           … Blown along by a cosmic wind…
               … You have already begun.

75. Blown along by a cosmic wind…
       … By the life-force of the universe…
           … Cradled by the spirit of unity…
               … You have already embarked…
                   … On the sacred journey of your life.

76. Within each, on life's pilgrimage...

    ... There is a receiver, always in tune...

        ... With the over-arching life force...

            ... With the wonderful spirit-wind...

            ... Of the sacred whole.

77. This vital connecting principle is known by some...

    ... As the human *'soul'*...

        ... Others call this precious jewel...

            ... Our *'true'*...

                ... Or *'higher'* Self.

78. Some call it *'Intuition'*...

        ... This unbreakable link with sacred knowledge.

Others deny it exists...

    ... Wisdom depends on it though.

79. Wisdom, called for at every moment...

    ... Is a matter of judgement, of discernment...

        ... That depends on maturity and experience.

For relevance, effectiveness and immediacy...

    ... It relies heavily too on *intuition*.

80. Wisdom depends on spontaneity...

   ... On readiness to speak or act...

      ... When the situation demands...

         ... On readiness too, sometimes...

           ... To remain silent and still.

ALERTNESS

81. Wisdom depends on alertness…

     … On being awake to the present moment.

     With no time for leisurely reasoning…

     … Lightning-fast intuition is key.

82. The present moment is everything…

     … As Greek philosophers of old were aware.

     The past has gone…

     … And the future has not yet arrived…

          … Everything that counts, happens *now*.

83. Buddhist lamas, Taoist sages…

     … Sufi saints, Hindu yogis…

          … Christian mystics…

                    … They all knew this to be true.

84. "Why worry about what you cannot alter?" the wise ones say.

Fix your thoughts on what happens elsewhere…

… On burdensome events of the past…

… Or possible calamities to come,

And your mind will surely be troubled.

85. Fix your mind on the present…

… On the immediacy of the *here and now*…

… Seeking at all times to act kindly,

And troubles will fall away…

… Leaving you joyful, at peace.

86. Here is a promise:

… When your mind is clear…

… And your heart is pure,

… You will dwell in a paradise…

… Upon the earth.

87. Here is an idea…

… The cast-iron truth of which…

… We must reveal within ourselves…

… That contentment and tranquillity…

… Grow (and grow only) with wisdom.

88. Whether believing, or not, this assurance…

   … We are wise to investigate, surely…

      … To seek out and discover…

                  … If all this might prove to be true.

   For what a great prize that would be!

EXPERIENCE, RATHER THAN BELIEFS

89. To be clear, wisdom depends on experience…

    … On judgement, and intuition.

    Surprisingly perhaps, it does *not* depend…

        … On beliefs or disbeliefs, about anything.

90. Wisdom depends upon experience…

    … On kindness, maturity, alertness…

        … And intuition…

            … Not on either religious or non-religious beliefs.

91. Not on theologies, then, does wisdom depend…

    … Neither on political or social ideologies.

    Such belief systems may help a person discover wisdom…

        … But, equally, (especially if divisive)…

            … They may not.

92. To be perfectly plain and simple...

    ... Wisdom brings harmony, not division...

        ... Fellowship, not discord...

                ... Otherwise, it is false.

93. Whatever separates people...

    ... Seeding conflict, enmity, hatred, and violence...

        ...Is not wisdom.

The wise count such things as folly.

WORLDLY AMBITION AND THE RISK OF HARM

94. Worldly desires, passions and ambitions…

    … For wealth, possessions, position, power…

        … And earthly pleasures,

  Are extremely hard to tame…

    … But they easily divide us from others.

95. Strive for success…

        … And have a good time when you like…

  But please be aware of the consequences…

        … Avoid harming yourself, or anyone else.

  That is a mature person's duty.

96. Being rich, famous or powerful…

    … Is perfectly fine…

        … As long as no-one is worse off…

            … In pain from our deeds or neglect.

97. Giving priority to riches, status, possessions…

　　… And taking control over people…

　　　… Leads quickly to rivalry and competition…

　　　　… Forging enemies…

　　　　　… Bringing strife to our door.

98. Seldom reliable…

　　… Worldly attractions like these…

　　　… Can only offer time-limited satisfaction…

　　　　… While breeding envy, mischief,
　　　　trouble, hostility…

　　　　　… Quarrels, cruelty and hatred.

99. Better than such fleeting goals…

　　… Is a determined ambition for wisdom…

　　　… Aiming to grow as a person…

　　　　… Throughout life.

VALUES AND VIRTUES

100. Growing, and gaining maturity...
    ... Involves acquiring personal attributes...
        ... The basic virtues that are bound up with wisdom...
            ... Of which there are many.

101. Based on deeply felt personal connections
    With the sacred unity of existence...
    ... With each other, with everyone else...
    The values and virtues of wisdom...
    ... Include kindness, patience and trust.

102. Universal kinship brings also...
    ... Perseverance, restraint, and tolerance...
        ... Gratitude and forgiveness...
            ... Honesty and humility.
    The list of virtues is long.

103. Contributing as well towards wisdom…

   … Are courage and compassion…

      … Generosity, devotion…

         … Love of beauty…

            … And hope.

104. *"Do as you would be done by"*…

   … This is the Golden Rule.

   Treat others, always, as you would wish to be treated…

   … Those you like *and* those you dislike.

   Such is the central message of wisdom.

105. "But how hard it is…

   … To treat well," I hear some say…

      … "The people that we dislike."

   I must agree…

   … And that precisely is why we need training.

WISDOM PRACTICE

106. It helps to read about wisdom…

    … To study ancient texts, scriptures and philosophy…

        … From all the world faiths and traditions…

            … Inscribed by the sages of old.

107. We do not have to believe to benefit…

    … Only to keep minds alert and open…

        … To learn and discover from poetry and literature…

            … From wise authors of recent times too.

108. Not to be led astray, though…

    … We need to gain experience…

        … To foster discernment…

            … And develop good judgement.

We must begin the *practice* of wisdom.

109. Wisdom practice, above all…

    … Involves learning how to be still…

        … To be still, silent…

            … And attentive to intuition…

                … To our most precious inner guide.

110. Some call the regular practice…

    … Of the 'wisdom exercise' of stillness…

        … 'Meditation', or, 'mindfulness'…

            … Or, 'prayer',

But I like the simple word *'stilling'*.

111. When learning to be still…

    … The basis of all wisdom practices…

        … It is good to have a teacher…

            … Also like-minded companions.

112. But, when no teacher or wisdom-friends are there…

    … Spend time quietly alone, every day…

        … Even for one minute…

            … Kneel, sit or lie down…

                … And be still.

113. This is how we become our own teachers…

    … With patience and perseverance.

One minute… Two minutes… Five minutes…

… Be quiet, even if you cannot be still…

… Watch mind and body gradually settle down.

114. Pay attention, moment by moment…

… As you engage with the stillness.

Distractions come and go…

… But there is no need to worry…

… Let them simply come… And let them go.

115. Arising out of our *passions*…

… Our likes and dislikes, hopes and fears…

Distracting sensations, thoughts…

… Emotions, and impulses…

… Come and go.

116. It is hard to master one's enthusiasms…

… Attachments and aversions, for and against…

… People, places, possessions…

… Activities and ideas…

Even for the wild products of our imagination.

117. Holding to strong likes and dislikes…

… Our passionate loves and hatreds…

…And the emotions they engender…

... Is the root cause...

... Of human suffering.

118. Taking responsibility for our passions...

... And our emotions...

... Can be hard,

Especially when they over-ride our best intentions...

... And that's why they have to be mastered.

119. Practice being still and silent.

Pay attention without holding tight...

... To sounds, ideas, strong feelings or urges...

... And your passions will be transformed...

... In tranquillity, into joy.

GROWING THROUGH ADVERSITY

120. Take time now to think for a minute…

  … About the nature of adversity…

    … About what makes us upset…

      … Brings us grief…

        … At the root of emotional pain.

121. Every life has ups and downs…

  … Misfortune and adversity cannot be avoided.

  Wisdom advises we profit by them…

    … Embrace them…

      … And use them to grow.

122. Of course we feel uncomfortable…

  … Facing strong challenges…

    … Whenever what's *'mine'* and *'ours'*…

      … Is under real, or imagined, threat.

123. Naturally we're unhappy…

  … When loss, damage or injury…

    … Affect anything that we cherish.

  Sometimes, we hold too to prejudice, loathing, detestation and hatred…

  … Causing ourselves further grief.

124. Facing *threat* to whatever we cherish…

  … We feel anxious and bewildered…

    … Full of doubt…

      … Often angry.

125. Facing *loss* brings likewise…

  … Irritation, annoyance…

    … And rage, as we try to resist.

  Loss may also bring shame and guilt upon us…

  … When thinking maybe we're to blame.

126. But, when loss becomes inevitable…

  … And what was held onto must finally be released…

    … We feel sad, lament, cry tears and wail.

  Accepting the pain, and letting grief's current flow free…

  … Is part of life's wisdom too.

127. The remedy for loss, it transpires…

 … Involves returning to stillness once more.
 Tranquillity, and the kindness of others…

  … Help the grieving process to flow.

128. Remaining tranquil…

 … Giving heartache full rein…

  … We will experience sadness weakening, dissolving…

   … And becoming transformed into joy.

129. And such everyday losses may be counted…

 … As valuable preparation for the day…

  … When each will be called to let go of life itself…

   … And, with it, all that we may ever have cherished.

130. To prepare for such finality,

 We are wise, early on, to examine all possible *threats*…

  … To seek out wherever we may be clinging too tightly…

   … By facing painful emotions…

    … And assenting to loss when we must….
 We can ready ourselves for the end.

131. By lamenting as nature intended, we prepare…

 … Crying our tears, letting go…

  … To experience the healing of nature…

... With doubt fading, confusion clearing...

   ... And the departure of fear.

132. Anger, on its release...

 ... liberates confidence and mental clarity...

  ... Letting peace and purity also return...

   ... Sorrow flies too...

    ... Leaving joy.

133. As shame and guilt fade also...

 ... Equanimity is restored, resilience bolstered...

  ... The healing process renewing strength, self-belief, maturity...

   ... Courage and hope.

134. Self-mastery and wisdom...

 ... Bring not only healing, but growth...

  ... Not by evading misfortune are we wise...

   ... But through facing and embracing...

    ... Adversity.

135. For, mastering our passions and emotions...

 ... In the face of losses and threat...

  ... Brings precious, hard-won experience...

   ... On life's perilous journey to wisdom.

LEARNING NEW SKILLS

136. How to prepare for dangers and hardship?

      With *skills*...

         ... Learned through gentle, regular practice.

      A firm but friendly routine of 'wisdom exercises'...

      ... Will help us grow and mature.

137. Wisdom exercises are effective...

      ... By strengthening our individual, indivisible sense of connection...

         ... To existence itself,

      The first skill is achieving stillness...

      ... Bringing full attention to our inner guide.

138. Stilling...

      ... Connecting us to the life-force of the universe...

         ... To nature, and to each other...

            ... Prepares us well for other practices...

               ... Promising wisdom.

139. Wisdom exercises to be adopted are...

    ... Aimed at staying healthy, in body and mind...

        ... Directed at the study of wisdom...

            ... Designed to promote our bonding with others...

                ... And engagement with the natural world.

140. Growing wiser, in addition...

    ... And closer to maturity, day by day...

        ... Helps a person increasingly to experience...

            ... Sacred unity, the divine...

                ... Which is bliss.

141. Wisdom exercises, for all to practice, include these...

    ... Physical and mental health promoting routines...

        ... Acts of kindness and service to others...

            ... Forging and fostering positive social relationships...

                ... And communing with marvels of nature.

142. Together with stilling...

    ... And studying wisdom...

        ... Build one or more of these...

            ... Into your daily routine...

                ... And you will soon feel yourself grow.

143. Taking exercise, and watching our diet,

    Avoiding toxins, and managing our weight…

        … Getting plenty of rest…

            … Including plenty of sleep…

                … All this will help us stay healthy.

144. Be pleasant, polite and welcoming…

    … Especially to strangers…

        … Offer kindness, care and companionship…

            … And all will soon become friends.

145. Sharing freely and generously every day…

    … Our possessions, money, and time…

        … Giving away (if nothing else)…

            … Lots of smiles…

This practice leads us to wisdom.

MORE WAYS TO GROW

146. It is surprising, amazing and wonderful...

   ... How joyful it can feel...

      ... To make a sacrifice...

         ... Doing something worthwhile and good...

           ... For someone who is in need.

147. Establishing and maintaining *loving* relationships...

   ... Within our families and communities...

      ... Involves a sometimes arduous kind of work.

Work, then, with tolerance, patience, gratitude and forgiveness...

   ... And surely all will be well.

148. There are countless ways of enjoying nature...

   ... Like growing plants, indoors or out...

      ... Walking in gardens and parks...

         ... In the country, in the mountains, and by the sea.

149. Paying attention to life, growth…

… Death and decay, teaches wisdom…

… Note the changing seasons and weather fluctuations…

… Observe magical landscapes, magnificent seascapes…

… And skies.

150. Walking, running, biking, sailing, swimming…

… Climbing, skiing, angling, golfing, and more…

… All may involve deploying and developing wisdom…

… Healing and making us whole.

151. Performed with skill and attention…

… Any mindfully engaged activity in nature …

… Offers excellent prospects of fine-tuning self-mastery…

… Fostering growth towards maturity and wisdom.

152. Other hobbies and pastimes work effectively too…

… Playing an instrument, learning to dance…

… Singing in a choir, for example…

… Joining with others to read or knit together…

… or play sport.

153. Remember wisdom's message though...

   ... In sport, as in business, politics, within families and
   elsewhere too...

      ... That winning and losing are far less important...

         ... Than sharing, playing your part...

            ... And keeping the welfare of
            others in mind.

154. Whatever fosters true fellowship...

   ... Self-control, humility...

      ... Loyalty and kindness...

         ... Must be good.

155. Whatever fosters creativity...

   ... In the service of others,

   Like art, and the performing arts...

   ... Has supreme value...

      ... Bringing harmony and wisdom to all.

156. Religious practices...

   ... Congregating for worship, sacred music and ritual...

      ... The reading of scripture...

            ... Going on pilgrimages and retreats,

   Work brilliantly well also for many.

157. Secular equivalent alternatives…

   … Festival celebrations…

      … Folk dancing, rites and traditions…

         … Literature and poetry reading,

Work superbly for others too.

EVERY ENDING IS A NEW BEGINNING

158. There is much more to be said…

    … About wisdom…

        … But this little book must end soon.

    Every ending is a new beginning…

        … You can always read it again.

159. Though more can be said about wisdom…

    … The very best teachers…

        … Are silence and stillness…

    Helping us each discover, and bring to life…

    … Our infallible inner guide.

160. Be still…

    … Be silent…

        … Pay attention…

            … Be kind…

                … And feel yourself grow.

More fruits of Larry's insightful meditations can be found in *The Big Book of Wisdom*, also published by Hero

Lightning Source UK Ltd.
Milton Keynes UK
UKHW050712270222
399045UK00018B/251